"To Be Free is Very Sweet": The Life of Mary Prince

A biography created by students from
Plant Hill Arts College, Plant Hill Rd, Blackley,
Manchester, M9 0WQ.

Students who contributed to this book:

Adam Lukoki

Abdul Ibrahim

Yosef Haile

Ayodele Alli

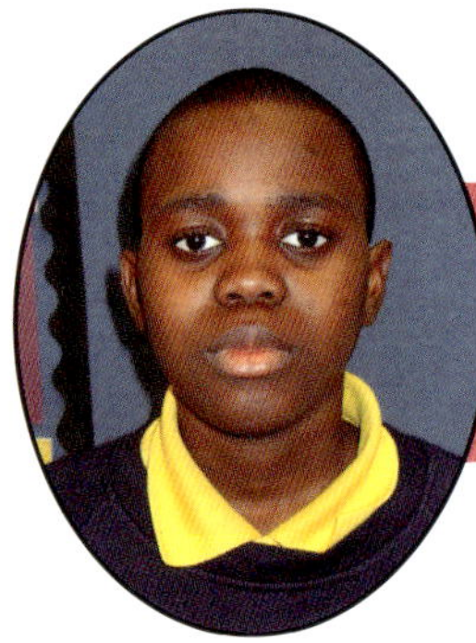

Hassan Bangura

Gemma Vaughan

Kieran Roche

Danielle Valente

Prologue:

In October 1562, a Devon ship's captain called John Hawkins led an expedition to the island of Tenerife. He'd already made arrangements with his Canary Island contacts to help him develop a trading enterprise that was new for the British: the slave trade. Guided by an experienced pilot, his four ships reached the Guinea coast where they fought and captured several Portuguese vessels filled with cargoes of cloves, wax, ivory and 400 enslaved Africans.

Hawkins sailed the captured vessels and their cargo across the Atlantic to the West Indies island of Espanola (present day Haiti and the Dominican Republic). Around half of the enslaved Africans died on the terrible journey. Those that survived were sold to Spanish planters. When Hawkins finally returned to Plymouth in the summer of 1563, his ships were loaded with Spanish coins, jewels and trade goods. The voyage was so profitable for its London investors that Queen Elizabeth I herself sponsored Hawkins' next slaving mission in 1564, making him a gift of a ship called the 'Jesus of Lubeck'.

British merchants soon came to dominate this barbaric trade in human beings. The capture and sale of enslaved Africans was incredibly profitable for these merchants until the official abolition of the trade in 1807. Over these 250 years, around 9.5million enslaved people were transported from Africa to the Americas. Millions more died during capture and transportation. This African holocaust was to have catastrophic consequences for the continent.

Slavery itself was not abolished in 1807. It would endure in the British colonies until much later in the century. Even after the passing of the Abolition of Slavery Act in 1833, the enslaved would endure more years of servitude under the new name of 'apprentice'. While the slave-owners received millions of pounds in compensation for their lost 'property', those who had suffered lifetimes of abuse received nothing.

Many slaves resisted by rebelling, running away, defying orders, forming banned relationships, supporting each other, developing their own cultural practices. The enslaved sought many ways to preserve body, soul and dignity. The quest for freedom was never-ending.

Mary Prince was a slave; she tried to resist the worst abuses of her 'owners' and did what she could to regain her freedom. The account of her experiences was written down in order to help the campaign against slavery. As Mary Prince proclaimed: **"To Be Free is Very Sweet."**

"Work – work – work – Oh that Turk's Island was a horrible place! The people in England, I'm sure, have never found out what is carried on there. Cruel, horrible place!...Oh the horrors of slavery! – How the thought of it pains my heart! But the truth ought to be told of it; and what my eyes have seen I think it is my duty to relate; for few people in England know what slavery is. I have been a slave – I have felt what a slave feels, and I know what a slave knows" (p.21)

Mary Prince, *The History of Mary Prince, A West Indian Slave, Related by Herself,* London, 1831; reprinted Penguin Classics, London, 2000, edited by Sara Salih

Mary was born in 1788 in Bermuda. Her father, Prince, worked as a sawyer (working with wood) in a ship-yard. He was enslaved. The name of her mother is unrecorded. She was a household slave to old Mr Myners.

When Mr Myners died, all of his property was divided or sold. The infant Mary and her mother were sold to the Williams family: harsh and selfish Captain Williams, master of a vessel that traded between America and the West Indies, whose return was dreaded by all; kind-hearted Mrs Williams, mistress of the family; and her only daughter Miss Betsey.

Miss Betsey was White and free; Mary was Black and enslaved. But the two girls were of similar age, and Mrs Williams was kind. In later years, Mary remembered this as *"the happiest period of my life....the tasks given out to us children were light, and we used to play together with Miss Betsey, with as much freedom almost as if she had been our sister." (p.7)*

Mary was contented, unaware of the days of toil and sorrow that lay ahead.

At the age of twelve, Mary was sent out to work for Mrs Pruden, who lived about five miles away from the Williams' house. Mary cried bitterly when she had to leave her mother, her brothers and sisters, her mistress and Miss Betsey. A few hours later, she found herself in a strange house among strange people. But her job was pleasant enough: she became nursemaid to the baby Daniel and loved to walk out with him by the seashore.

Within this household, Mary again found kindness. Miss Fanny, sister of baby Daniel, was

> *"so fond of me that she wished me to learn all that she knew herself; and her method of teaching me was as follows:- Directly she had said her lessons to her grandmamma, she used to come running to me, and make me repeat them one by one after her; and in a few months I was able not only to say my letters but to spell many small words." (p.9)*

For a few months, Mary stayed with the Pruden family, her happiness only marred by the sudden death of Mrs Williams, for whom she wept.

Gemma Vaughan

Then Mary was given terrible news. Captain Williams was to be married again and, to pay for his wedding, Mary and two of her sisters would be sold.

Mary's mother was powerless to stop this and even had to take her own daughters to the market-place as though they were chickens!

> *"We followed my mother to the market-place where she placed us in a row against a large house, with our backs to the wall…I as the eldest, stood first, Hannah next to me, then Dinah; and our mother stood beside, crying over us. My heart throbbed with grief and terror so violently, that I pressed my hands quite tightly across my breast, but I could not keep it still and it continued to leap as though it would burst out of my body. …At length the vendue master who was to offer us for sale like sheep or cattle arrived…He took me by the hand and led me out into the middle of the street, and, turning me slowly round, exposed me to the view of those who attended…I was soon surrounded by strange men, who examined and handled me in the same manner that a butcher would a calf or lamb." (p.11)*

Mary was sold for 57 Bermuda pounds. She and her sisters were sold to different masters; parted forever from their mother and from each other.

Gemma Vaughan
Kieran
Danielle Valente

Mary soon discovered that her new masters were very cruel. As she entered the yard, two slave women cried out "Poor child, poor child, you must keep a good heart if you are to live here". Her new mistress, Mrs I- , told her off for crying. The only person to show Mary kindness was another slave called Hetty. Mary was terrified when, later that night, she heard Hetty cry out as she was violently beaten by Captain I-. Mary trembled with terror, thinking it was her turn next.

The next day, Mary's new mistress began her instructions:

> *"She taught me to do all sorts of household work; to wash and bake, pick cotton and wool, and wash floors and cook. And she taught me (how can I ever forget it!) more things than these; she caused me to know the exact difference between the smart of the rope, the cart-whip, and the cow-skin when applied to my naked body by her own cruel hand. And there was scarcely any punishment more dreadful than the blows I received on my face and head from her hard heavy fist. She was a fearful woman, and a savage mistress to her slaves." (p14)*

Too slow! Go faster!
Cruel wicked whip slashes skin;
Deep scars: 'Shame on you.'

Haiku by the boys.

For five years, Mary received almost daily beatings. She often tried to resist: challenging the reasons for the ill-treatment of herself and others. Once, Mary ran away to her mother, who hid her daughter in a cave because she dared not let her in the house. There was nowhere Mary could safely go and anyone caught helping her would be severely punished. Eventually, her father took her back to Capt I- and pleaded with him to be more kind in future.

> *"Sir, I am sorry that my child should be forced to run away from her owner; but the treatment she has received is enough to break her heart. The sight of her wounds has nearly broke mine. I entreat you, for the love of God, to forgive her for running away, and that you will be a kind master to her in future." (p18)*

Mary's father could do little more than plead for better treatment for his daughter; even this was risky and dangerous for him, and might provoke brutal punishment. Loving parents faced the torture of being able to do little to protect their children from fearful abuse.

20th July 1800

Wanted

Run away

Girl named Mary Prince,

13years.

Two pounds 15 shillings reward for

taking her to gaol.

Last seen on road to Brackish

Pond

Where her mother lives.

Runaway advert by the boys.

Around 1805, Mary was sold to Mr D- of Turk's Island. She was not allowed to say goodbye to any of her family before she set off on the four week sea-voyage. When food provisions ran short, Mary was saved from starvation by *"the kindness of a black man called Anthony and his wife, who had brought their own victuals, and shared them with me". (p.19)*

Mr D- had Mary valued: she was now worth 100 Bermuda pounds. As soon as they arrived, Mary was put to work in the salt ponds at Grand Quay. This work involved raking up the salt from seawater ponds. The workers were exposed to the fierce sun as well as standing in salty water all day long. This caused terrible and painful boils on their feet and legs.

Mary described their night quarters:

> *"We slept in a long shed, divided into narrow slips, like the stalls used for cattle. Boards fixed upon stakes driven into the ground, without mat or covering, were our only beds." (p.19)*

Mary's mother was brought to Turk's island, but by this time, her mother had 'lost her senses' and did not recognise Mary. While she was on the island, Mary also heard that her father had died. She was very alone.

WANTED

29 December 1812,

RUNAWAY!

A NEGRO GIRL,

MARY PRINCE, about 24 years old, has no brand mark. She ran away in 1812, and has never been seen.

TWO POUNDS SEVENTEEN SHILLINGS AS A REWARD.

Take her to any gaol of this island.

Runaway advert by the boys.

For ten years Mary suffered in the salt ponds of Turk's Island. Then Mr D- retired, and took Mary with him, back to Bermuda. There she worked in the grounds, planting and tending sweet potatoes, Indian corn, plantains, bananas, cabbages, pumpkins and onions. She did all the household chores, ran errands for Mr D- and his daughters, and tended to the animals – a horse and a cow. With so much work, Mary was rarely still, but still she rejoiced that Turk's Island was behind her.

One day, Mary returned from fetching water and came across Mr D- drunk and violently beating his daughter. Mary intervened, and pulled the girl away from her father. When Mr D- went to attack her instead, she challenged him and said: *"Sir, this is not Turk's Island".*

> *"I then told him I would not live longer with him, for he was a very indecent man – very spiteful and too indecent; with no shame for his servants, no shame for his own flesh. So I went away to a neighbouring house and sat down and cried till next morning, when I went home again, not knowing what else to do." (p.24)*

"Last week my father got drunk and, as usual, was rude and aggressive. I felt scared, frightened – I tried to get away. I started to cry and scream when he hit me with his hard fist. He is so horrible. I wondered where Mary was – would she come and help me like she has done before? She is brave, standing up to my father. I know she will protect me if she can. I can trust Mary: she is selfless, generous and true." Miss D-

Imaginative writing by the boys.

Hot, salty island;
Backbone hurting, blistered feet;
Exhausted, no rest.

Haiku by the boys.

In 1815, when Mary was around 27 years old, she was sold to Mr and Mrs John Wood for 100 Bermuda pounds. They lived in Antigua and Mary was taken on as a household servant and nursemaid. However, Mary became very ill with rheumatism and a serious illness called 'St Anthony's fire' (erysipelas) which meant she was crippled for several months. She was left lying in an out-house, with little attention from her new mistress. Her only comfort at this time came from a fellow slave who brought her herbal medicines to bathe in.

Over the next few years Mary continued to work for the Woods, but was often at odds with them. She was determined to save any money she could make.

"The way in which I made money was this - When my master and mistress went from home, as they sometimes did, and left me to take care of the house and premises, I had a good deal of time to myself and made the most of it. I took in washing and sold coffee and yams and other provisions to the captains of ships. I did not sit still idling during the absence of my owners; for I wanted, by all honest means, to earn money to buy my freedom." (p.27)

Gemma Vaughan

In 1817, Mary was baptized into the Anglican Church, but she soon converted to the Moravian Church, which was much more sympathetic to the enslaved. It was the Moravians who taught Mary to read the Bible. It was in the Moravian church that Mary was married to Daniel James, a free carpenter and cooper (barrel-maker), in 1826. Slaves could not be married in the Anglican Church and neither could a free man marry a slave woman.

Daniel James had purchased his freedom some years before. Mr & Mrs Wood were very angry with Mary for getting married and would not let her husband on their premises. At this time, Mary again asked the Woods if she could buy her freedom, but they refused:

> *"Mrs Wood was very angry – she grew quite outrageous – she called me a black devil and asked me who had put freedom into my head. 'To be free is very sweet', I said: but she took good care to keep me a slave." (p.31)*

Danielle Valente

In 1828, Mary went to London with the Woods. She was now around 40 years old. She hoped that her ill-health might improve in London, and also that the Woods might finally let her buy her freedom, so that she could return to Antigua a free woman. Again, Mary was let down. Furthermore, after so many years of abuse, Mary struggled to complete her work because she was too ill for the heavy laundry duties required of her.

In November, the Woods threatened to put her out on the street. Mary again asked to buy her freedom and was again refused. She was scared to leave of her own accord as she had no friends or support in London. Eventually, after being threatened with eviction for the fourth time, Mary decided she could take no more. She left the Woods and asked the Moravian Missionaries for help.

For a while, Mary stayed with a sympathetic family called Mash. Mr Mash worked cleaning & sharpening knives and repairing shoes. Mrs Mash was a laundress. Although poor themselves, they did all they could to support Mary. When she was a little better, Mrs Mash helped her find work as a charwoman (cleaning and odd jobs).

Finally, at the end of November 1828, Mary made her way to the Anti-Slavery Society in Aldermanbury, London. The Society gave her a little money to support herself, but they also gave her disappointing news: they told Mary that *"the laws of England could do nothing to make me free in Antigua" (p. 35).* If Mary returned to her husband in Antigua, the Woods could reclaim her as a slave.

Members of the Anti-Slavery Society themselves offered Mr Wood money to buy Mary's freedom, but still he refused. Mary was trapped in London. For a few months Mary worked as a domestic servant for a Mrs Forsyth, until, in 1829, she went to work for Martha and Thomas Pringle. Thomas Pringle was the secretary of the Anti-Slavery Society. He understood that Mary's account of her life in slavery could be a valuable tool in the anti-slavery campaign. Mary's testimony was written down in a book. It was the first life of a Black woman published in Britain.

"In telling of my own sorrows, I cannot pass by those of my fellow-slaves – for when I think of my own griefs, I remember theirs." (p.22)

In 1829, the Anti-Slavery Society presented a petition to Parliament on Mary's behalf. In 1831, Mary's testimony of her life story, written down by Susanna Strickland, was published and printed in three editions. Thomas Pringle paid for the printing. Mary's book was read by members and sympathisers of the Anti-Slavery Society across Britain. Moreover, the scarring and marks of serious floggings on Mary's body were seen and described by Mrs Pringle, and several other ladies. They wrote letters that supported Mary's account and sent these to women's organisations involved in the campaign against slavery.

Mary's testimony: *A History of Mary Prince, A West Indian Slave, related by herself,* gave people a clear account of the horrors of slavery. Many people in Britain wanted this unjust system to end and Mary's account helped them in their campaign.

In 1833, Mary was called to speak in two lawsuits that were prompted by her testimony. A publisher called Thomas Cadell of *Blackwood's* magazine printed an article that claimed Thomas Pringle had manipulated Mary for his own purposes. Mary argued that she had given the account of her life freely, and the case was won by Pringle. But in the next lawsuit, John Wood sued Thomas Pringle for libel. Although Mary spoke on his behalf, Pringle lost this case and was ordered to pay £25 damages to Wood.

The account of Mary Prince's life past 1833 cannot be completed. She disappeared from public view, and we do not know what happened to her. Even the date of her death is unknown.

But slavery in the British colonies was coming closer to its end. Partly thanks to Mary's testimony, the Abolition of Slavery Act was passed by the British Parliament in 1833 to become effective in 1834. While the legacy of slavery would be long-lasting, Mary had fought and won her battle to bear witness for her people.

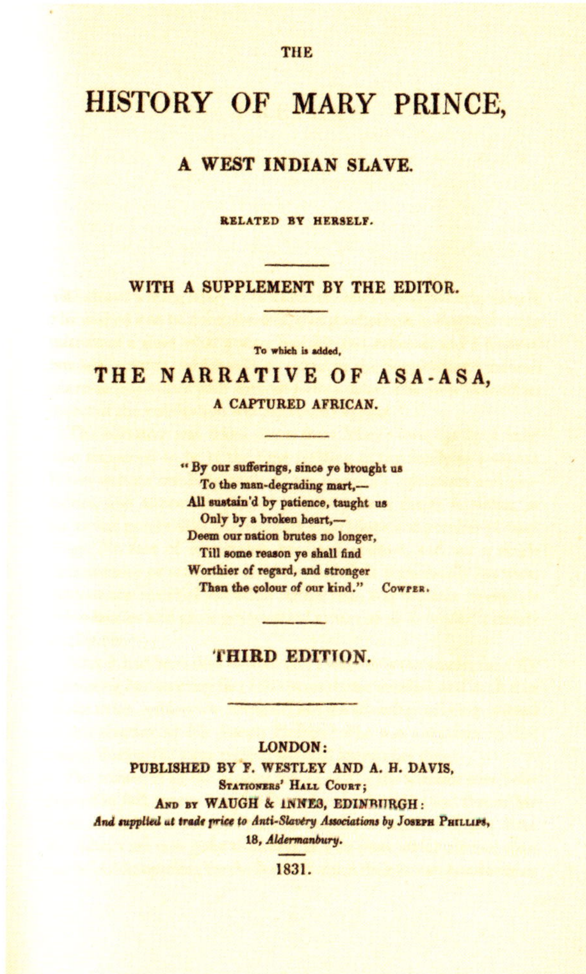

THE

HISTORY OF MARY PRINCE,

A WEST INDIAN SLAVE.

RELATED BY HERSELF.

WITH A SUPPLEMENT BY THE EDITOR.

To which is added,

THE NARRATIVE OF ASA-ASA,

A CAPTURED AFRICAN.

"By our sufferings, since ye brought us
To the man-degrading mart,—
All sustain'd by patience, taught us
Only by a broken heart,—
Deem our nation brutes no longer,
Till some reason ye shall find
Worthier of regard, and stronger
Than the colour of our kind." COWPER.

THIRD EDITION.

LONDON:
PUBLISHED BY F. WESTLEY AND A. H. DAVIS,
STATIONERS' HALL COURT;
AND BY WAUGH & INNES, EDINBURGH:
And supplied at trade price to Anti-Slavery Associations by JOSEPH PHILLIPS,
18, *Aldermanbury.*

1831.

Mary Prince - a Timeline

DATE	
c1788	Mary Prince is born in Brackish Pond, Bermuda. Sold to Captain Darrel for his grandchild Betsey Williams.
c1800	Aged 12, Mary is sent out to work for Mrs Pruden, working as a nursemaid, looking after baby Daniel. Sold by public auction and separated from her mother and siblings. Moves to the house of her new master Capt and Mrs I- and is often beaten. Runs away but is brought back as there is nowhere else to go.
c1805	Sold to Mr D and sent to work in the salt ponds at Grand Quay, Turk's Island. (In 1807, the Abolition of the Slave Trade is passed in Britain but does not end slavery in the Caribbean).
c1812	Mr D retires to Bermuda and takes Mary to work at household chores, looking after the animals and growing crops. Mary defends Miss D against her father's beating. Mary stands up to him and runs away, but again has to go back as there is nowhere she can go.
1815	Sold to Mr and Mrs John Wood of Antigua for £100 (Bermuda currency). Works as a washerwoman in Antigua – her rheumatism is very severe and she also develops a disease called 'St Anthony's fire' (erysipelas) meaning she is disabled for several months.

Mary Prince - a Timeline

DATE	
1815	Mary is supported by a fellow slave, who provides herbal medicines. Tries to save money by working when the Woods are away from home by taking in washing and selling provisions. Mary asks several times if she can buy her freedom – but the Woods persistently refuse.
1817	Baptized into the Anglican Church but begins to attend the Moravian Church which is more sympathetic to the enslaved, and is taught to read the bible.
1826	Mary marries Daniel James, a free carpenter and cooper in the Moravian Chapel, Spring Gardens, Antigua, but without the permission or agreement of Mr and Mrs Wood. Mary again asks the Woods if she can buy her freedom, but they refuse.
1828	Taken to London by the Woods. Mary struggles to complete her work. In November the Woods threaten to put her out. Mary again asks if she can buy her freedom and is again refused. After receiving the threat of being put out four times, she walks out and asks for help from the Moravian Missionaries. Stays for a while with a family called Mash who help Mary to find work as a charwoman (cleaning and odd jobs).
1828	Goes to the Anti-Slavery Society in Aldermanbury, London and receives some money. The Society offers Mr Wood money to buy Mary's freedom, but he refuses.

Mary Prince - a Timeline

DATE	
1829	Works for Mrs Forsyth as a domestic servant, for around six months.
1829	Enters domestic service with Martha and Thomas Pringle. Thomas is the secretary of the Anti-Slavery Society. He presents a Petition to Parliament on Mary's behalf.
1829-1831	Mary dictates her life to Susanna Strickland. It is published as a book by the Anti-Slavery Society. The scars on Mary's body are seen by some of the ladies of the Anti-Slavery Society. Mary's testimony includes this statement: "All slaves want to be free – to be free is very sweet."
1833	Testifies in two law-suits: Pringle's suit against publisher Thomas Cadell of *Blackwood's* magazine, for slander (won); and John Wood's lawsuit against Thomas Pringle for libel. (In 1833 The Slave Emancipation Act is passed by the British Parliament and will bring about the ending of slavery in the Caribbean from 1838).

The date of Mary's death is unknown.
We also do not know if she was ever able to return to her husband in Antigua.

Glossary:

Apprentice: a person learning a skilled trade from someone else.

Arrangements: a plan for a future event.

Barbaric: savagely cruel.

Bear witness: describe the events you have seen take place.

Catastrophic: an event causing great damage or suffering.

Contacts: people you are in touch with, who can help you.

Enterprise: a business project.

Holocaust: destruction or slaughter/killing on a mass scale.

Investors: people who put money into a project with the expectation of making a profit.

Pilot: a person with local knowledge who is able to take charge of a ship entering or leaving a harbour.

Planters: managers or owners of a plantation, which is a large estate on which crops such as coffee, sugar and tobacco are grown.

Preserve: keep safe from harm or in its original state.

Testimony: a formal statement, especially if given in a court of law, which acts as evidence or proof.

Transported: carried from one place to another by means of a vehicle, in this case a ship.

Servitude: the state of being enslaved, of being completely controlled by someone more powerful.

Vendue master: like an auctioneer, someone heading up a sale.

Individual Credits and Sources used as a Stimulus for Art and Writing:

'The boys': Ayodele Alli, Hassan Bangura, Yosef Haile, Abdul Ibrahim and Adam Lukoki. Year 10 Art students :Kieran Roche, Danielle Valente and Gemma Vaughan.

pv. *Map of the Triangular Trade, created by the boys* with reference to sources in the National Maritime Museum pack FREEDOM, A History and Citizenship KS3 resource to investigate the Transatlantic Slave Trade; and to design ideas on historic maps.

p2. *Old Street in Bermuda, painted by Gemma.* From an image by Frank Black, 'Back Street Bermuda', c1932, on website S83.photobucket.com

p4. *Mary and child, painted by Gemma.* From an un-credited image used in The Guardian, October 2007 to illustrate the article "They bought me as a butcher would a calf or lamb" by Sara Wajid.

p6. *Separation of Families, drawn by Kieran.* From an etching by W.Skelton, 1787, image card 2a in the FREEDOM pack.

p8. Whips used against people on plantations are on various image cards in the FREEDOM pack.

p8. *Haiku created by the boys*, after discussion of brutal punishments inflicted on the enslaved.

p10 & 12. *Runaway adverts, created by the boys* with reference to the many examples to be found e.g. on www.spartacus.schoolnet.co.uk

p13. The boys imagined what Miss D might think about Mary helping her in the face of her father's abuse.

p14. *The Island Seaview, painted by Gemma.* From an image by E.de Berard, 'The Bermudas', c1860, on website www.anthonypettit.com/prints